AWESOME DOGS

Greyhounds

by Lindsay Shaffer

BELLWETHER MEDIA • MINNEAPOLIS, MN

Note to Librarians, Teachers, and Parents:

Blastoff! Readers are carefully developed by literacy experts and combine standards-based content with developmentally appropriate text.

Level 1 provides the most support through repetition of high-frequency words, light text, predictable sentence patterns, and strong visual support.

Level 2 offers early readers a bit more challenge through varied simple sentences, increased text load, and less repetition of high-frequency words.

Level 3 advances early-fluent readers toward fluency through increased text and concept load, less reliance on visuals, longer sentences, and more literary language.

Level 4 builds reading stamina by providing more text per page, increased use of punctuation, greater variation in sentence patterns, and increasingly challenging vocabulary.

Level 5 encourages children to move from "learning to read" to "reading to learn" by providing even more text, varied writing styles, and less familiar topics.

Whichever book is right for your reader, Blastoff! Readers are the perfect books to build confidence and encourage a love of reading that will last a lifetime!

This edition first published in 2019 by Bellwether Media, Inc.

No part of this publication may be reproduced in whole or in part without written permission of the publisher. For information regarding permission, write to Bellwether Media, Inc., Attention: Permissions Department, 6012 Blue Circle Drive, Minnetonka, MN 55343.

Library of Congress Cataloging-in-Publication Data

Names: Shaffer, Lindsay, author.
Title: Greyhounds / by Lindsay Shaffer.
Description: Minneapolis, MN : Bellwether Media, Inc., 2019. | Series:
   Blastoff! Readers. Awesome Dogs | Audience: Age 5-8. | Audience: K to
   Grade 3. | Includes bibliographical references and index.
Identifiers: LCCN 2018031877 (print) | LCCN 2018037517 (ebook) | ISBN
   9781681036397 (ebook) | ISBN 9781626179080 (hardcover : alk. paper)
Subjects: LCSH: Greyhounds--Juvenile literature.
Classification: LCC SF429.G8 (ebook) | LCC SF429.G8 S53 2019 (print) | DDC
   636.753/4--dc23
LC record available at https://lccn.loc.gov/2018031877

Editor: Betsy Rathburn   Designer: Laura Sowers

Printed in the United States of America, North Mankato, MN.

Table of Contents

What Are Greyhounds?

Greyhounds are super fast dogs. They can reach speeds of more than 40 miles (64 kilometers) per hour!

These dogs are quiet and **affectionate**. They love to cuddle!

Long, Lean Bodies

Greyhounds have **lean**, muscular bodies. Their tails are thin and curved.

sprinting

Long legs help
greyhounds **sprint**!

Greyhounds have long
snouts. Their heads are
narrow with small, folded ears.

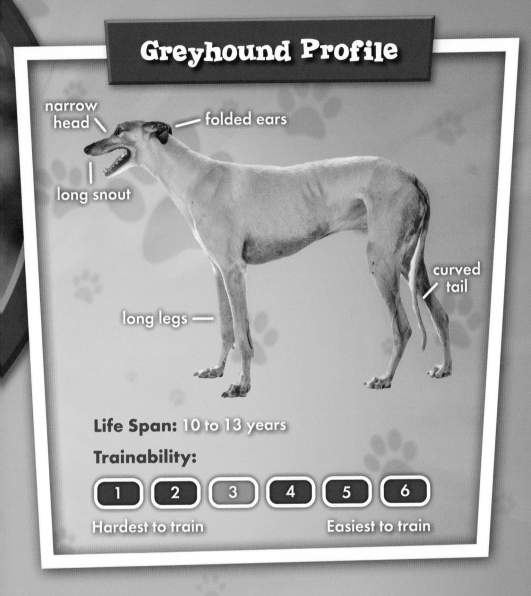

Greyhound Profile

narrow head

folded ears

long snout

curved tail

long legs

Life Span: 10 to 13 years

Trainability:

1 | 2 | 3 | 4 | 5 | 6

Hardest to train   Easiest to train

This **breed** can weigh up to 70 pounds (32 kilograms). They grow more than 2 feet (0.6 meters) tall!

brindle

Greyhound **coats** come in many different colors. Red, white, **fawn**, and black are common.

Greyhound Coats

spotted

solid

Coats may be **solid** or spotted. Some coats are **brindle**.

11

History of Greyhounds

Thousands of years ago, greyhounds lived in Egypt. **Pharaohs** trained them as hunting dogs.

Egypt →

Later, European kings and
queens kept greyhounds.

Explorers brought the dogs to the Americas in the 1500s. They quickly spread to the United States!

In 1885, greyhounds joined the **American Kennel Club** as part of the **Hound Group**.

Couch Potatoes

Greyhounds are calm and **easygoing**. They enjoy short sprints followed by long naps.

Greyhounds are known
for being couch potatoes!

Long legs make it hard for greyhounds to sit. They prefer to lie down or stand.

Soft blankets and pillows
help them lie down in comfort.

Greyhounds make gentle family pets. They enjoy relaxing indoors.

These sweet dogs are as loving as they are fast!

Glossary

affectionate—loving

American Kennel Club—an organization that keeps track of dog breeds in the United States

breed—a type of dog

brindle—a solid coat color mixed with streaks or spots of another color

coats—the hair or fur covering some animals

easygoing—calm and free of worries

fawn—a light brown color

Hound Group—a group of dog breeds that often have a history of hunting

lean—thin

pharaohs—rulers of Egypt from long ago

snouts—dogs' noses

solid—one color

sprint—to run at top speed

To Learn More

AT THE LIBRARY

Bozzo, Linda. *I Like Greyhounds!* New York, N.Y:
Enslow Publishing, 2017.

Gagne, Tammy. *The Dog Encyclopedia for Kids.*
North Mankato, Minn.: Capstone Young Readers,
2017.

Gagne, Tammy. *Foxhounds, Coonhounds, and Other
Hound Dogs.* North Mankato, Minn.: Capstone
Press, 2017.

ON THE WEB

FACTSURFER

Factsurfer.com gives you
a safe, fun way to find
more information.

1. Go to www.factsurfer.com.

2. Enter "greyhounds" into the search box.

3. Click the "Surf" button and select your
   book cover to see a list of related web sites.

Index

The images in this book are reproduced through the courtesy of: Eric Isselee, front cover, pp. 11, 12; Liliya Kulianionak, pp. 4-5; Kate Grishakova, pp. 5, 8-9, 10-11, 14; Nodnitram, pp. 6-7; Grigorita Ko, pp. 7, 11; Dan Kosmayer, p. 9; Hulton Fine Art Collection/ Getty, p. 13; Fireglo, p. 15; BiancaGrueneberg, pp. 16-17, 21; Clearvista, p. 17; SvetaElfimova, pp. 18-19; Paige V. Polinsky, p. 19; Myrleen Pearson/ Alamy, pp. 20-21.